ALLEN JACKSON
Pastor, World Outreach Church

Defeating Fear with God's Love, Purpose, and Power

FREEDOM FROM
WORRY

OVERCOMING ANXIETY

Six-Week Video Study

FREEDOM FROM WORRY

OVERCOMING ANXIETY

Defeating Fear with God's Love, Purpose, and Power

Table of Contents

FREEDOM FROM WORRY

Overcoming Anxiety with God's Love, Purpose, and Power

Introduction

The Aussies have a great expression: "Neau warries!" ("No worries!" in a down under accent).

The Jamaicans have a catchy tune behind one of their cultural philosophies: "Don't worry! Be Happy!" Too many people use the same tune with the words, "I'm worried! And unhappy!"

But have you ever heard someone say, "The thing that impresses me most about Christians is that they live without worry"?

I'm sad to say I haven't heard us described that way. And yet Jesus said some very pointed things about worry, the main one being that He didn't want us to do it! He gave us very good reasons not to worry, and He offered great and practical alternatives to worry. In fact, if our lives are characterized by worry, then it's fair to say we either don't know what Jesus said about it, or we are deliberately choosing to disobey Him and ignore His promises. I'm hoping it's more a case of ignorance than disobedience for most of us.

In this study, we're going to discover that too often we've settled with worry as a constant companion, when it doesn't have any good place in our lives. Because the feelings connected with worry are powerful, they leave us with the illusion that when we worry we're actually accomplishing something. In reality, we're taking time and energy away from what we should be doing, while we waste time worrying. We accomplish nothing of value at all!

I realize you might have to take my word for it right now, but good things are ahead for you as you learn to show worry out the door of your life. I can promise you, based on the Word of God, that if you will engage with others in this study, you will discover a significant and life-altering *freedom from worry* as you learn to live life Jesus' way.

Using This Workbook

Here are some tips to help you have a great small group experience!

Notice in the Table of Contents there are three sections: (1) Sessions, (2) Appendix, and (3) Small Group Leaders. Familiarize yourself with the Appendix. Some parts of it will be used in the sessions themselves.

If you are facilitating/leading or co-leading a small group, the section Small Group Leaders will give you some hard-learned experiences of others that will encourage you and help you avoid many common obstacles to effective small group leadership.

Use this workbook as a guide, not a straightjacket. If the group responds to the lesson in an unexpected but honest way, go with that. If you think of a better question than the next one in the lesson, ask it. Take to heart the insights included in the Frequently Asked Questions pages and the Small Group Leaders section.

Enjoy your small group experience.

Read the outline of each session on the next pages so that you understand how the sessions will flow.

Outline of Each Session

Most people want to live a worry-free life, but few achieve this by themselves. And most small groups struggle to balance all of God's purposes in their meetings. Groups tend to overemphasize one of the various reasons for meeting. Rarely is there a healthy balance that includes teaching, evangelism, ministry, practical exercises, and worship. That's why we've included all of these elements in this study so you can live a healthy, balanced spiritual life over time.

A typical group session for *Freedom from Worry* will include the following:

STORY

The lessons we will learn during *Freedom from Worry* are best illustrated in the lives of real people. Each session will begin with a summary of someone's story, and the video presentation during the session will capture firsthand that person telling their story.

GETTING STARTED

The foundation for spiritual growth is an intimate connection with God and His family. A few people who really know you and who earn your trust provide a place to experience the life Jesus invites you to live. This section of each session typically offers you two options. You can get to know your whole group by using the icebreaker question(s), or you can check in with one or two group members—your spiritual partner(s)—for a deeper connection and encouragement in your spiritual journey.

DVD TEACHING SEGMENT

Serving as a companion to the *Freedom from Worry* small group discussion book is the *Freedom from Worry* video teaching. This DVD is designed to combine teaching segments from Pastor Allen Jackson with leadership insights and personal stories of life change. Using the teaching video will add value to this six-week commitment of doing life together and discovering how walking with Christ changes everything.

(NOTE: If time is limited, discuss bold questions first.)

DISCUSSION

This section is where you will process as a group the teaching you heard and saw. The focus won't be on accumulating information but on how we should live in light of the Word of God. We want to help you apply the insights from Scripture practically, creatively, and from your heart as well as your head. Allowing the timeless truths from God's Word to transform our lives in Christ is our greatest aim.

APPLICATION

We let the truth we are learning travel the eighteen inches from our cranium (mind) to our cardium (heart, emotions, and will) in this portion. This is where the Bible instructs us to "be doers of the Word, not just hearers" (James 1:22). Many people skip over this aspect of the Christian life because it's scary, relationally awkward, or simply too much work for their busy schedules. But Jesus wanted all of His disciples to help outsiders connect with Him, to know Him personally, and to carry out His commands. This doesn't necessarily mean preaching on street corners. It could mean welcoming a few newcomers into your group, hosting a short-term group in your home, or walking through this study with a friend. In this study, you'll have an opportunity to go beyond Bible study to biblical living.

DEEPER BIBLE STUDY

If you have time and want to dig deeper into more Bible passages about the topic at hand, we've provided additional passages and questions. Your group may choose to do study homework ahead of each meeting in order to cover more biblical material. If you prefer not to do study homework, the Deeper Bible Study section will provide you with plenty to discuss within the group. These options allow individuals or the whole group to expand their study, while still accommodating those who can't do homework or are new to your group.

FREEDOM FROM WORRY

Overcoming Anxiety with God's Love, Purpose, and Power

DAILY DEVOTIONALS

Each week on the Daily Devotionals pages we provide Scriptures to read and reflect on between group meetings. We suggest you use this section to seek God on your own throughout the week. This time at home should begin and end with prayer. Don't get in a hurry; take enough time to hear God's direction.

WEEKLY MEMORY VERSES

For each session we have provided a Memory Verse that emphasizes an important truth from the session. This is an optional exercise, but we believe that memorizing Scripture can be a vital part of filling our minds with God's will for our lives. We encourage you to give this important habit a try.

Session 1

Worry: Jesus' Opinion

The truth is, most of us don't feel like we need to be introduced to worry. We know it quite well. In fact, we may have to be introduced to the idea that we can actually experience freedom from worry. That's the good news here at the start of our study! Let's agree we are going to join forces in the weeks to come to make worry a stranger in our lives.

Story

Amber Gray

The cover on a book may or may not give us some accurate clues about the contents of its pages. The way a person looks or presents themselves in a moment may not tell us much about where they have been and how they got to this place. Amber Gray is a lovely, soft-spoken young wife and mother of three. She appears to be someone who could apply to be the poster child for a carefree life. And yet, there's a lot more to her story.

Amber is honest about the opportunities to worry that are continually before a young mother. Because she wants to be a great mom, she often finds herself overwhelmed. But she has learned to use the temptation to worry as a reminder to trust. Whether it's the step of faith to leave her kids behind while she and her husband took a life-changing trip to Israel, or simply going about her busy daily schedule as a mom, she knows that every day will present her with tests and choices about worry.

We will also see that some of her current challenges relate to her upbringing. The stability of her life today has not erased the impact of difficult lessons growing up. Amber has a lot to share with those who .

may feel like they are alone, confused, and broken. She's been there. And she can share what God does in a life with all that baggage to make it a life that displays His glory. He turned a self-described "church-gypsy" into a grown woman who understands God's presence in her life and is eager to share her hope with others.

Amber and her two oldest children have memorized Psalm 91 together, an amazing description of what it means to live a worry-free life that includes God's promise about how He treats those who trust Him. If you have time, read this psalm before the session.

Getting Started

We will begin each session with a question or brief activity designed to "put us on the same page." Since this is your first time together (at least for this new series), take a few minutes to make sure everyone knows each other's names.

 What comes to mind when you hear the word "worry"?

 Describe a situation in your life that you would admit is likely to provoke you to worry.

FREEDOM FROM WORRY

Overcoming Anxiety with God's Love, Purpose, and Power

DVD Session #1

Throughout the sessions in *Freedom from Worry* we're going to be hearing some pointed teaching from Pastor Allen Jackson as well as some personal stories from people who have wrestled with worry and discovered a measure of freedom. With that possibility in mind, let's begin our teaching for this session.

I. General Principles of Worry-Free Living

Hebrews 12:1-3

¹ *Therefore, since we are surrounded by such a great cloud of witnesses, let us throw off everything that hinders and the sin that so easily entangles, and let us run with perseverance the race marked out for us.*

² *Let us fix our eyes on Jesus, the author and perfecter of our faith, who for the joy set before him endured the cross, scorning its shame, and sat down at the right hand of the throne of God.*

³ *Consider him who endured such opposition from sinful men, so that you will not grow weary and lose heart.*

A. No unnecessary _____

B. Run with _____ = endurance

C. Christ-centric: Jesus changes _____

    1. Endured the _____

    2. Rejected _____

    3. Overcame _____

II. Jesus Teaches about Worry

Matthew 6:25-34

²⁵ "Therefore I tell you, do not worry about your life, what you will eat or drink; or about your body, what you will wear. Is not life more important than food, and the body more important than clothes?

²⁶ "Look at the birds of the air; they do not sow or reap or store away in barns, and yet your heavenly Father feeds them. Are you not much more valuable than they?

²⁷ "Who of you by worrying can add a single hour to his life?

²⁸ "And why do you worry about clothes? See how the lilies of the field grow. They do not labor or spin.

²⁹ "Yet I tell you that not even Solomon in all his splendor was dressed like one of these.

³⁰ "If that is how God clothes the grass of the field, which is here today and tomorrow is thrown into the fire, will he not much more clothe you, O you of little faith?

³¹ "So do not worry, saying, 'What shall we eat?' or 'What shall we drink?' or 'What shall we wear?'

³² "For the pagans run after all these things, and your heavenly Father knows that you need them.

³³ "But seek first his kingdom and his righteousness, and all these things will be given to you as well.

FREEDOM FROM WORRY
Overcoming Anxiety with God's Love, Purpose, and Power

[34] *"Therefore do not worry about tomorrow, for tomorrow will worry about itself. Each day has enough trouble of its own."*

Philippians 4:6-7
[6] *Do not be anxious about anything, but in everything, by prayer and petition, with thanksgiving, present your requests to God.*

[7] *And the peace of God, which transcends all understanding, will guard your hearts and your minds in Christ Jesus.*

    A. Conclusion: Worry is a _____

    B. Impact: Worry will _____ God's best for your life.

Mark 4:18-19
[18] *"Still others, like seed sown among thorns, hear the word;*

[19] *but the worries of this life, the deceitfulness of wealth and the desires for other things come in and choke the word, making it unfruitful."*

Discussion

Using the questions that follow, we will review and expand on the teaching we just experienced. If time is limited, discuss bold questions first.

3 Pastor Allen began his teaching with the point that we face a world of continuous and sometimes overwhelming change. What changes in the last few years have affected your life the most?

4 When change does occur (and we all agree that it does happen), what are some of the good and bad ways that we respond or react to change?

5 What stood out for you in the way Amber talked about dealing with worry in her life? Why?

6 After reading the passage from Hebrews 12:1-3, Pastor Allen highlighted three principles of living based on the example of Jesus. The first principle was: Don't carry unnecessary baggage through life. In addition to worry, identify some forms of baggage we might carry.

FREEDOM FROM WORRY

Overcoming Anxiety with God's Love, Purpose, and Power

7 People frequently picture life as a race, but what kind of race is it for you? Between "heavy" and "weightless," how would you describe the load you're carrying in the race right now?

8 **Principle two was about the need to run the race with perseverance/endurance. What does the term "perseverance" mean to you? How did you identify with Pastor Allen's admission that he wishes this wasn't one of the requirements of the Christian life?**

9 The third principle from Hebrews 12:1-3 is huge: Jesus changes everything. If the logical conclusion based on Jesus' life and His teaching is that worry is sin, how does that truth change the way you handle worry?

10 Philippians 4:6 says, *Do not be anxious about anything, but in everything, by prayer and petition, with thanksgiving, present your requests to God.* In what practical ways is prayer a resolution to worry?

Application

Now it's time to make some personal applications of all we've been thinking about in the last few minutes.

11 **Of the three life-lessons from Hebrews 12:1-3, 1) lose the baggage, 2) keep moving, and 3) eyes on Christ, which one is the most immediate challenge in your life? Why?**

12 **Mark 4:18-19 says, "*Still others, like seed sown among thorns, hear the word; but the worries of this life, the deceitfulness of wealth and the desires for other things come in and choke the word, making it unfruitful.*" How have you found it true that the presence of worry in your life drowns out and chokes the Word?**

13 How do you see this small group experience pushing you toward greater consistency in pursuing *freedom from worry*?

FREEDOM FROM WORRY

Overcoming Anxiety with God's Love, Purpose, and Power

14 Pastor Allen ended his teaching with the challenge to think of others who are struggling with worries that we might invite to join us for these sessions. If someone came to mind, write their name(s) here:

15 What's one choice you can make this week (and share with the group) that you believe would move you toward exercising greater *freedom from worry*?

16 Allow everyone to answer this question: How may we pray for you this week? Write this week's prayer requests on this page and make note of them on the Prayer & Praise Report on page 89. As you progress through the study, thank God for the ways He is working in the lives of your group members.

Close the session in prayer. Pray for others in the group. Use the following prayer as you end this session:

Heavenly Father, today I choose to follow the path You have marked out for me—may Your will be done in my life. I need Your help. When I am weary, renew my strength. When I am distracted, by Your grace redirect my attention. Holy Spirit, help me to recognize anything that hinders my progress. In Jesus' name, amen.

Prayer Requests:

_____
_____
_____
_____
_____
_____
_____
_____
_____
_____

Going Deeper Bible Study
Personal Devotion & Reflection

You can explore the following Bible passages behind the teaching for this session as a group (if there is time) or on your own between sessions.

Read Matthew 6:25-34. This is the most extensive teaching Jesus gave on the subject of worry. It includes great reasons not to worry, as well as good practices to use when responding to worry.

- How many different points of worry does Jesus mention in this passage? How many are matters you worry about?

- What are some of the things Jesus points out that are unhelpful and even harmful about worry (there are at least seven)?

- Verses 26, 28, 33, and 34 each include at least one alternative to worry. Describe them and discuss how practicing them would make a difference in the matters you worry about.

FREEDOM FROM WORRY
Overcoming Anxiety with God's Love, Purpose, and Power

Read Hebrews 12:1-3 again and 1 Corinthians 9:24-27. Paul is using some of the same imagery applied by the writer of Hebrews to compare the disciplines of the Christian life to the pattern of training for and running a race.

- In Greek, the phrases "run with perseverance," "endured the cross," and "endured such opposition" all use the same root word *hupomone*, which also related to patience, waiting, and training. The word literally means to "stay under." Instead of trying to escape the limitations, frustrations, or delays in situations, try to stay under the weight until we gain something from carrying it. How is worry a subtle way to try to escape the weight of life?

- In athletics, every race has a certain training regimen—we don't train the same for the 100-yard dash as we do for a marathon, though both involve running. What kind of life training do you think makes a significant difference when it comes to the things we worry about?

- Pastor Allen talked about "baptizing worry" with code words like "concern," "prayer request," "discernment," and "sharing." We learn three things in Philippians 4:6-7: (1) present your requests to God, (2) cast your cares, (3) give thanks. Have you spent more time this week following this advice or worrying? Explain.

Daily Reflections

These are daily reviews of the key Bible verses and related Scriptures that will help you think about and apply the insights from this session.

Day 1 – Philippians 4:6
Real *Freedom from Worry*
Do not be anxious about anything, but in everything, by prayer and petition, with thanksgiving, present your requests to God.
Reflection Question: How do thanksgiving and anxiety coexist in the same heart? Which one are you letting rule?

Day 2 – Matthew 6:25
The Worry-Free Life
"Therefore I tell you, do not worry about your life, what you will eat or drink; or about your body, what you will wear. Is not life more important than food, and the body more important than clothes?"
Reflection Question: How do you answer Jesus' question?

Day 3 – Matthew 6:31-32
Running the Wrong Way
"So do not worry, saying, 'What shall we eat?' or 'What shall we drink?' or 'What shall we wear?' For the pagans run after all these things, and your heavenly Father knows that you need them."
Reflection Question: "How might your life change if you stopped running after the things Jesus mentioned?"

Day 4 – Matthew 6:34
Living Today

"Therefore do not worry about tomorrow, for tomorrow will worry about itself. Each day has enough trouble of its own."

Reflection Question: Does good planning involve worrying about tomorrow, or is good planning an alternative to worrying about tomorrow? If so, how?

Day 5 – Mark 4:18-19
Pulling Weeds

"Still others, like seed sown among thorns, hear the word; but the worries of this life, the deceitfulness of wealth and the desires for other things come in and choke the word, making it unfruitful."

Reflection Question: What specific worries do you want to see God pull from your life during this study so you can be free to follow His Word?

Weekly Memory Verse:

Do not be anxious about anything, but in everything, by prayer and petition, with thanksgiving, present your requests to God.

Philippians 4:6

Session 2

Freedom to Live

Welcome to week two of **Freedom from Worry!** *This time we get to meet two more fellow travelers seeking the Kingdom of God. And we get to think about the fact that God wants us to leave worry behind so that we can truly live. Enjoy the conversations.*

Story

Chuck and Michelle Zingale

Twenty-four years of marriage and three sons are two significant notes in a couple's "experience" profile. Because a husband and wife have different tendencies and strengths, it's easy for a couple to unconsciously develop individual focus, becoming quite unaware of what their partner is doing day-to-day as they zero in on their own role. Like many couples, Michelle's specialty was home and kids; Chuck's was work and providing for the family.

As we will see, God didn't let that compartmentalized life go unchallenged. He used various means to wake Chuck and Michelle up to the fact that marriage, and life with Him, is a team effort. Now they both have insights to offer regarding the way worry drives us away from, or toward, God.

Chuck and Michelle are quick to note that, even though they have come a long way in learning to trust God, the practice of trust, and the discipline of choosing not to worry, is a daily challenge. Our capacity for worry isn't something we retire. We can't start fudging on Jesus' words about worry, claiming that we get to worry about the little/unimportant things, but we'll trust Him with the big things.

Chuck and Michelle have discovered in different ways that God wants to be trusted in everything. As Chuck puts it, "What I've chased or worried about on my own in life I have lost; what God has given has remained." Michelle added, "I've not only had to learn not to worry; I've had to learn how important it is to lighten up!"

Getting Started

We will begin each session with a question or brief activity designed to "put us on the same page." Continue to make sure everyone knows each other's names.

1 One of the concepts that will come up in this session is the fact that everything in our lives (including us) has an expiration date. When you open your refrigerator, what products would you say you are most likely to check the expiration date on before you use them? Why? Any stories connected with that caution?

2 As a benefit for those who might be joining us for the first time, what insight from last week have you been applying that you would be willing to mention to the rest of the group?

FREEDOM FROM WORRY
Overcoming Anxiety with God's Love, Purpose, and Power

DVD Session #2

Throughout the sessions in *Freedom from Worry* we're hearing some pointed teaching from Pastor Allen Jackson, as well as some personal stories from people like Chuck and Michelle, who have lived with the challenge of Christ's freedom in life. The circumstances of our lives vary, but we all can choose to follow Jesus' directions for living. With that possibility in mind, let's begin our teaching for this session.

I. Word History (etymology) of WORRY

In Old English: to _____
In Middle English: to grasp by the _____ (the way wolves might attack sheep)
16th century: to _____ or _____
Currently: to feel _____, _____, or _____

II. Jesus' Comments on Worry

Matthew 6:25-34
25"Therefore I tell you, do not worry about your life, what you will eat or drink; or about your body, what you will wear. Is not life more important than food, and the body more important than clothes?

26"Look at the birds of the air; they do not sow or reap or store away in barns, and yet your heavenly Father feeds them. Are you not much more valuable than they?

27"Who of you by worrying can add a single hour to his life?

28"And why do you worry about clothes? See how the lilies of the field grow.

They do not labor or spin.

[29]"Yet I tell you that not even Solomon in all his splendor was dressed like one of these.

[30]"If that is how God clothes the grass of the field, which is here today and tomorrow is thrown into the fire, will he not much more clothe you, O you of little faith?

[31]"So do not worry, saying, 'What shall we eat?' or 'What shall we drink?' or 'What shall we wear?'

[32]"For the pagans run after all these things, and your heavenly Father knows that you need them.

[33]"But seek first his kingdom and his righteousness, and all these things will be given to you as well.

[34]"Therefore do not worry about tomorrow, for tomorrow will worry about itself. Each day has enough trouble of its own."

A. Inappropriate _____

    1. Temporal—beneath the sun

Ecclesiastes 2:22-23
[22] What does a man get for all the toil and anxious striving with which he labors under the sun?

[23] All his days his work is pain and grief; even at night his mind does not rest. This too is meaningless.

Summary of Jesus' Teaching: Do Not _____!

   B. Appropriate _____ . . . Unusual Perspective

    1. Eternal—ultimate issues

Matthew 6:33-34

[33] *But seek first his kingdom and his righteousness, and all these things will be given to you as well.*

[34] *Therefore do not worry about tomorrow, for tomorrow will worry about itself. Each day has enough trouble of its own.*

Matthew 10:16, 26-28

[16] *"I am sending you out like sheep among wolves. Therefore be as shrewd as snakes and as innocent as doves . . .*

[26] *"So do not be afraid of them, for there is nothing concealed that will not be disclosed, or hidden that will not be made known.*

[27] *"What I tell you in the dark, speak in the daylight; what is whispered in your ear, proclaim from the roofs.*

[28] *"Do not be afraid of those who kill the body but cannot kill the soul. Rather, be afraid of the One who can destroy both soul and body in hell."*

III. Why is Worry Damaging?

Mark 4:18-19

[18] *"Still others, like seed sown among thorns, hear the word;*

[19] *but the worries of this life, the deceitfulness of wealth and the desires for other things come in and choke the word, making it unfruitful."*

At best, it distracts our _____

At worst, it causes our faith to be _____

Matthew 13:22

[22] *"The seed falling among the thorns refers to someone who hears the word, but the worries of this life and the deceitfulness of wealth choke the word, making it unfruitful."*

FREEDOM FROM WORRY
Overcoming Anxiety with God's Love, Purpose, and Power

Discussion

Using the questions that follow, we will review and expand on the teaching we just experienced. If time is limited, discuss bold questions first.

 Pastor Allen began this session with a word study on *worry*. The history is a combination of what worry *means* and what worry *does*. Discuss ways that worry chokes, and diminishes effectiveness in your life.

Reviewing Jesus' comments about anxiety in Matthew 6:25-34, Pastor Allen noted this: "Jesus didn't say that the matters He mentioned (like food and clothing) weren't important; He said these matters are an inappropriate concern." What is an inappropriate concern? What are some other examples?

What was your personal takeaway from Chuck and Michelle's story?

6 How did you understand Pastor Allen's statement that Jesus' summary command about worry, "Don't do it," means among other things, we don't *have* to worry?

7 In drilling down on the destructiveness of worry, Pastor Allen made two observations: 1) Worry distracts our focus until our eyes are off God, and 2) Worry drains the meaning and fruitfulness out of life. How do these two destructive tendencies work together to tear down someone's life?

8 The Bible makes it clear that the first correct response when we realize we have been doing something wrong is to repent. Are you carrying worries that you are willing to lay down and embrace repentance? Are there any you can share?

Application

Now it's time to make some personal applications of all we've been thinking about in the last few minutes.

9 Pastor Allen reminded us from Matthew 6:33-34 that Jesus expects us to "seek first His kingdom and His righteousness." What does this dual command mean in your life today?

10 One of the danger signs about worry mentioned in this session is being alert for "what drains enthusiasm out of life." What concerns have you discovered that have this draining effect on your relationship with God?

11 Matthew 13:22 teaches us that the "worries of this life" can come in and "choke the Word." In contrast, how does God's Word help you choke out worry?

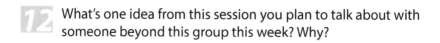

12 What's one idea from this session you plan to talk about with someone beyond this group this week? Why?

13 As you think about this next week, in what ways can you apply Michelle's point that worry and fear-based decisions are usually wrong.

FREEDOM FROM WORRY
Overcoming Anxiety with God's Love, Purpose, and Power

Close the session in prayer. Pray for others in the group. Use the following prayer as you end this session:

Heavenly Father, I entrust myself to Your care. I purposefully lay aside each point of anxiety and fear. Thank You that Your angels are watching over my life. May Your peace fill my heart. You are my refuge and my strength. In Jesus' name, amen.

Prayer Requests:

_____

_____

_____

_____

_____

_____

_____

_____

_____

_____

Going Deeper Bible Study
Personal Devotion & Reflection

You can explore the following Bible passages behind the teaching for this session as a group (if there is time) or on your own between sessions.

Read Luke 10:38-42. Jesus stayed in Mary and Martha's home regularly. The two sisters and their brother Lazarus were His friends. They participated in several significant events in Jesus' ministry, including the raising of Lazarus from the dead (John 11:1-44) and one of Jesus' final meals (John 12:1-11).

- Based on verse 40, what would you say was "necessary" and what was an unhealthy distraction in this situation?

- How would you express Martha's sentiment to Jesus in your own words?

- Read Jesus' response to Martha and then discuss what would have been the healthiest and most fruitful lesson Martha could have taken from that situation. Does John 12:1-11 indicate that either Martha or Mary or both may have learned something from this exchange?

FREEDOM FROM WORRY

Overcoming Anxiety with God's Love, Purpose, and Power

Daily Reflections

These are daily reviews of the key Bible verses and related Scriptures that will help you think about and apply the insights from this session.

Day 1 – Mark 4:18-19

Hearing Limits

"Still others, like seed sown among thorns, hear the word; but the worries of this life, the deceitfulness of wealth and the desires for other things come in and choke the word, making it unfruitful."

Reflection Question: What "worries of life" do you need to address fearlessly this week?

Day 2 – Luke 10:42

One Thing Needed

"But only one thing is needed. Mary has chosen what is better, and it will not be taken away from her."

Reflection Question: What is the "one thing" you want to focus on this week that expresses your desire to love God more openly?

Day 3 – Ecclesiastes 3:11

Seeing Beauty

He has made everything beautiful in its time. He has also set eternity in the hearts of men; yet they cannot fathom what God has done from beginning to end.

Reflection Question: How does choosing to focus on God and what He has done put everything we worry about in perspective for you?

Day 4 – Matthew 6:33-34

Looking for His Kingdom

"But seek first his kingdom and his righteousness, and all these things will be given to you as well. Therefore do not worry about tomorrow, for tomorrow will worry about itself. Each day has enough trouble of its own."

Reflection Question: If you are going to seek His Kingdom by looking for evidence of God at work around you, what will you be looking for tomorrow as you go about your day?

Day 5 – Matthew 10:28

No Fear

"Do not be afraid of those who kill the body but cannot kill the soul. Rather, be afraid of the One who can destroy both soul and body in hell."

Reflection Question: How is fear connected to worry in your life, and what areas of fear do you need to turn over to the only One worth fearing in all of life?

FREEDOM FROM **WORRY**

Overcoming Anxiety with God's Love, Purpose, and Power

Weekly Memory Verse:

"But seek first his kingdom and his righteousness, and all these things will be given to you as well. Therefore do not worry about tomorrow, for tomorrow will worry about itself. Each day has enough trouble of its own."
(Matthew 6:33-34)

Session 3

Pathway to Worry-Free Living

If the Gospels are any indication of a pattern, Jesus'
priorities today would be distinctly contrary to what
everyone else is talking about. As He did so often, He would
move right past the superficial and direct His attention to
the bigger issues inside us that really occupy most of our
time and provoke most of our worries. Jesus had a way of
getting to the heart of matters.

Story

Seth Kolka

The father-son relationship has a powerful effect
on a young man growing up. The early loss of that
relationship, as Seth discovered with the tragic
death of his dad when he was in high school, can
have far-reaching impact on a son's development
and approach to manhood.

For Seth, his father's death left a void filled with
fears, doubts, and questions with seemingly no
answers. But he also discovered that God has a
way of using people to edge into the void. Seth
now sees that God provided key men, in His
timing, to give direction. He also learned he didn't
have to have all of the answers in order to trust
God. Like many before him, Seth is discovering
that answers, like "stuff" we depend on, easily
come to replace God as the thing we trust. If our
answers are challenged or fall apart, we're back
where we started. God wants us to trust Him, even
when the answers run out or are not immediately
available.

A decade-and-a-half after his dad's death, Seth still finds his father
an example in many ways. He is a father himself now. Whether he's
thinking about raising his own daughter, continuing to relate to his
younger brother and sister, or considering how to run his chiropractic

practice and ministry opportunities, Seth has found an even greater source of direction and comfort in God his Father.

Seth will be the first to point to God in the middle of crisis and remind himself and us, "Take a breath, pause, and renew your trust in God . . . because fear and worry are a waste of time!"

Getting Started

We will begin each session with a question or brief activity designed to "put us on the same page." Continue to make sure everyone knows each other's names.

1 Have each person rank the following list 1 to 10 based on what they think is the order of things people worry about the most:

_____ Global warming
_____ Crime
_____ Aging
_____ Favorite sports team
_____ Stock market
_____ Family
_____ Health/Weight
_____ Terrorism
_____ Employment
_____ Health insurance

FREEDOM FROM WORRY
Overcoming Anxiety with God's Love, Purpose, and Power

Identify the top three according to your group's answers. Since worrying is not a practical approach to any of these matters, what does the group think would be the best and healthiest alternative response?

2 On behalf of those who might be joining us for the first time this session, who would like to describe one significant discovery you've made since we began these sessions on *Freedom from Worry*?

DVD Session #3

Throughout the sessions in *Freedom from Worry* we're hearing some pointed teaching from Pastor Allen, as well as some personal stories from people like Seth Kolka, who is on the adventure of worry-free living. Each week we are taking a hard look at worry in order to drive it from our lives so we can live the way God wants us to live. With that objective in mind, let's begin our teaching for this session.

I. Jesus' Unique Perspective
Matthew 6:28-33

^{28}"And why do you worry about clothes? See how the lilies of the field grow. They do not labor or spin.

^{29}"Yet I tell you that not even Solomon in all his splendor was dressed like one of these.

^{30}"If that is how God clothes the grass of the field, which is here today and tomorrow is thrown into the fire, will he not much more clothe you, O you of little faith?

^{31}"So do not worry, saying, 'What shall we eat?' or 'What shall we drink?' or 'What shall we wear?'

^{32}"For the pagans run after all these things, and your heavenly Father knows that you need them.

^{33}"But seek first his kingdom and his righteousness, and all these things will be given to you as well."

    A. What is not addressed: (social justice, politics)

    B. The heart of the matter, focus of worry is

_____

   C. The remarkable invitation: choosing a different life path.

II. God's Provision

John 14:26-27
[26]"But the Counselor, the Holy Spirit, whom the Father will send in my name, will teach you all things and will remind you of everything I have said to you.

[27]"Peace I leave with you; my peace I give you. I do not give to you as the world gives. Do not let your hearts be troubled and do not be afraid."

   A. Presence of the _____ _____

John 16:12
[12]"I have much more to say to you, more than you can now bear."

   B. Peace in the midst of _____

   C. The gift of God's Spirit brings: _____, _____, and _____ of mind.

2 Timothy 1:7
[7] For God did not give us a spirit of timidity, but a spirit of power, of love and of self-discipline.

III. Maintaining a Trust Transfer

Zechariah 4:6
[6] So he said to me, "This is the word of the LORD to Zerubbabel: 'Not by might nor by power, but by my Spirit,' says the LORD Almighty."

   A. In relationship with _____

   B. Welcome the _____ _____

   C. Recognize your _____

Proverbs 4:23
[23] Above all else, guard your heart, for it is the wellspring of life.

Discussion

Using the questions that follow, we will review and expand on the teaching we just experienced. If time is limited, discuss bold questions first.

3 Have a volunteer read Matthew 6:25-34. The objective is to find as many of the seven specific personal matters Jesus mentioned in His comments on worry. List as many as you can here:

1._____

2._____

3._____

4._____

5._____

6._____

7._____

4 How have you seen in your own life the reality of God's timing in providing help that Seth talked about?

5 **What are some "personal issues" that people often avoid talking about that they nevertheless worry about?**

6 We heard in the video "If you can't trust God with the common necessities of life, it's absurd to think you will trust Him with your eternal destiny." How does this challenge you?

FREEDOM FROM WORRY

Overcoming Anxiety with God's Love, Purpose, and Power

7 After quoting John 14:27, *"Peace I leave with you; my peace I give you. I do not give to you as the world gives. Do not let your hearts be troubled and do not be afraid,"* what did Pastor Allen say about it not being enough to read and understand these words of Christ?

8 In introducing the pathway to a worry-free life, Pastor Allen included the crucial need for 1) the Holy Spirit's presence, and 2) Christ's peace even in the middle of conflict. How does the Holy Spirit help you be peaceful in the midst of tumultuous circumstances?

Application

Now it's time to make some personal applications of all we've been thinking about in the last few minutes.

9 In a relationship with God we learn to trust Him more fully. Think of a persistent fear in your life. What would it look like to trust God in that arena? Explain.

10 The Holy Spirit is our Counselor/Helper. How would you like to trust Him more today?

11 In a turbulent world we are constantly bombarded with troubling thoughts. List two to three things you can do to guard your heart and mind.

12 What experiences have you had in talking with others outside the group about what we are studying together during these sessions? How is your *freedom from worry* affecting others in your life?

Close the session in prayer. Pray for others in the group. Use the following prayer as you end this session:

Heavenly Father, I rejoice today because You are my provider. I am Your child, and You are aware of all my needs. I thank You that You are Lord over my circumstances. Your grace and power are sufficient to meet all my concerns. Today I give You all my anxiety and frustration. I choose Your peace. Holy Spirit, help me to be content, to trust and to yield to Almighty God. I choose to turn my thoughts toward the majestic Kingdom of my Lord and rest in His provision. In Jesus' name, amen.

Prayer Requests:

_____

_____

_____

_____

_____

_____

_____

_____

_____

FREEDOM FROM WORRY
Overcoming Anxiety with God's Love, Purpose, and Power

Going Deeper Bible Study
Personal Devotion & Reflection

You can explore the following Bible passages behind the teaching for this session as a group (if there is time) or on your own between sessions.

Read John 14:23-27. Jesus was urgently offering His example and His words as the hours wound down on His mission to planet earth. He was keenly aware that the disciples would not understand much of what He was saying and doing, but He was confident that the "Counselor, the Holy Spirit" would fill the gaps in their memories and comprehension.

- Although the Bible never uses the term Trinity to describe God, this is one of those passages in which each person of the Godhead has an interlocking role to play. What are those roles?

- What characteristics of Jesus' peace are mentioned in these verses? Identify at least three.

- Verses 23-24 paint a sobering picture of how Jesus evaluates our statements of love for Him. Given the standard in those verses, how does your love stack up?

Jesus gave us a personal journal for defeating anxiety:

- Verse 23 – How is our love for Jesus expressed?

- Verse 26 – What are two things the Holy Spirit will do for us?

- Verse 27 – Jesus left us with what? What did Jesus tell us not to do?

- Jesus' life was not free of conflict or struggles, yet He maintained peace. Similarly, our lives are often touched with conflict and struggles. Take a few moments and list the places today where you are feeling challenged.

- Now ask the Holy Spirit to direct you toward the peace of our Lord.

These are daily reviews of the key bible verses and related Scriptures that will help you think about and apply the insights from this session.

Day 1 – Zechariah 4:6
By the Spirit
So he said to me, "This is the word of the LORD to Zerubbabel: 'Not by might nor by power, but by my Spirit,' says the LORD Almighty."
Reflection Question: What regular activity in your life do you normally pursue in your own strength and power? What difference would it make to approach it by God's Spirit in you?

Day 2 – Ephesians 1:13-14
Sealed
And you also were included in Christ when you heard the word of truth, the gospel of your salvation. Having believed, you were marked in him with a seal, the promised Holy Spirit, who is a deposit guaranteeing our inheritance until the redemption of those who are God's possession—to the praise of his glory.
Reflection Question: How would you describe your current awareness of the Holy Spirit's presence in your life as God's seal?

Day 3 – Proverbs 4:23
A Guarded Heart
Above all else, guard your heart, for it is the wellspring of life.
Reflection Question: How exactly are you going about posting a guard over your life?

Day 4 – 2 Timothy 1:7

Empowering Spirit

For God did not give us a spirit of timidity, but a spirit of power, of love and of self-discipline.

Reflection Question: Which of these three gifts from God (power, love, self-discipline) do you find most lacking in your actions today? How have you made this a matter for prayer?

Day 5 – John 14:26

Indwelling Counselor

"But the Counselor, the Holy Spirit, whom the Father will send in my name, will teach you all things and will remind you of everything I have said to you."

Reflection Question: To what degree is the absence of worry in you directly connected to your awareness of the Holy Spirit's presence?

Weekly Memory Verse:

Above all else, guard your heart, for it is the wellspring of life.

(Proverbs 4:23)

Session 4

God's Remedy for Worry

By this session we should be settling into a level of comfort with the group, continuing to welcome any newcomers. In this session we will take a look at some biblical strategies for avoiding and removing worry from our lives. When we have good alternatives, the temptation to worry won't be nearly as strong!

Story

Ross Bradley

There is something astoundingly authentic about a man wearing a mechanic's overalls, a business suit, or a uniform while speaking with quiet passion about his relationship with God. Pastors are expected to teach and preach, but men in particular are often led to Christ and grow in Christ under the influence of other men. Ross Bradley speaks as an ordinary man who is continually discovering new ways to follow and trust an extraordinary God.

In almost a replay of a biblical story, Ross was invited to go on a fishing trip during a time when he was dealing with tremendous financial pressures. Since his business relies on securing large amounts of money for financing building projects, the extreme downturn in the market was cause for worry. And yet God used a raccoon to show Ross a picture of how the process of working and depending on God go together. We can't do everything, but God does want us to do something.

As a young father working to keep his marriage strong, Ross has discovered that an important component of intimacy is praying together. Though counterintuitive in a human sense, the idea of attraction based on spiritual growth and caring has a strong biblical precedent. God wouldn't direct men to lead their families spiritually if there were not other benefits that came with the role. Ross and his wife have discovered that God's blessings have encouraged them to share with others.

Ross recognizes the importance of men backing up one another. Though tempted to approach problems individually, a man who

depends on brothers, and offers them his support, is in the long run a greater masculine model than the man who fails alone and has no companions to sustain him. Men are at their best when they can focus on one thing. Ross likes to point out that we almost always have a choice before us between trusting God or paying attention to our problems. We can't do both at the same time. His vote is for trusting God every time.

Getting Started

We will begin each session with a question or brief activity designed to "put us on the same page." Continue to make sure everyone knows each other's names.

1 Take a minute or two to think about different ways you would complete the following sentence: If I had more *freedom from worry*, I would have more freedom to _____. Have several people in the group share.

2 Since we are now embarking on the second half of this study, let's take a moment to share what's been significant for us personally as we've thought in this extended way about worry.

DVD Session #4

Throughout the sessions in *Freedom from Worry* we're hearing some pointed teaching from Pastor Allen Jackson as well as some personal stories from people like Ross Bradley, who has lived free from worry. With that thought in mind, let's begin our teaching for this session.

I. God's Remedy for Worry

    A. Examine your _____

        1. Legitimate responsibilities grow into obstructions.

Luke 10:41-42
41"Martha, Martha," the Lord answered, "you are worried and upset about many things,

42"but few things are needed—or indeed only one. Mary has chosen what is better, and it will not be taken away from her."

        2. Correlation between worry and the desire for wealth

Mark 4:18-19
18"Still others, like seed sown among thorns, hear the word;

19"but the worries of this life, the deceitfulness of wealth and the desires for other things come in and choke the word, making it unfruitful."

Matthew 6:24
24"No one can serve two masters. Either you will hate the one and love the other, or you will be devoted to the one and despise the other. You cannot serve both God and money."

    B. Learn to _____

Philippians 4:6-7
⁶ Do not be anxious about anything, but in everything, by prayer and petition, with thanksgiving, present your requests to God.

⁷ And the peace of God, which transcends all understanding, will guard your hearts and your minds in Christ Jesus.

   C. God is _____

Hebrews 4:15-16
¹⁵ For we do not have a high priest who is unable to empathize with our weaknesses, but we have one who has been tempted in every way, just as we are—yet he did not sin.

¹⁶ Let us then approach the throne of grace with confidence, so that we may receive mercy and find grace to help us in our time of need.

   D. Give the problem to _____

1 Peter 5:7
⁷ Cast all your anxiety on him because he cares for you.

   E. Live one _____ at a time.

Matthew 6:34
³⁴ Therefore do not worry about tomorrow, for tomorrow will worry about itself. Each day has enough trouble of its own.

John 21:20-22
²⁰ Peter turned and saw that the disciple whom Jesus loved was following them. (This was the one who had leaned back against Jesus at the supper and had said, "Lord, who is going to betray you?")

²¹ When Peter saw him, he asked, "Lord, what about him?"

²² Jesus answered, "If I want him to remain alive until I return, what is that to you? You must follow me."

FREEDOM FROM WORRY
Overcoming Anxiety with God's Love, Purpose, and Power

Discussion

Using the questions that follow, we will review and expand on the teaching we just experienced. If time is limited, discuss bold questions first.

3. What are some boundaries we can establish even around our legitimate responsibilities and roles in life to keep them from becoming obstructions in our relationship with God?

4. The Bible does not condemn wealth; in fact, abundance is a blessing from God. However, Jesus said wealth is deceptive (will cause you to believe something that is untrue). Discuss some ways wealth is deceptive.

5. **Explain the difference between being content and being complacent. Paul wrote in Philippians 4:12, *I know what it is to be in need, and I know what it is to have plenty. I have learned the secret of being content in any and every situation, whether well fed or hungry, whether living in plenty or in want.* How do you think he learned that lesson of contentment?**

6. **The second step in accepting God's remedy for worry is learning to pray. Describe one practice you have learned in the Christian life that has significantly improved your prayer life. How is listening a significant part of a healthy prayer life?**

7   How does the fact that God really knows what we're going through, according to Hebrews 4:15, make a difference for you when it comes to trusting God with the things you worry about?

Application

Now it's time to make some personal applications of all we've been thinking about in the last few minutes.

8   **The opening words of 1 Peter 5:7 are,** *Cast all your anxiety on him…* **Pastor Allen suggested making a list, balling it up, and throwing it away. Take time now to make your list using the note pages in the appendix on page 105. Tear the list out and take turns throwing those recorded anxieties away.**

9   **Worry is often fueled by concerns about tomorrow. Let's each make a proclamation: Today I am trusting God for**

_____.

10   Read Hebrews 4:16. A time of need is not a weakness, but an opportunity to experience God. Is there a need in which you would welcome expressions of God's grace and mercy? Explain.

11   In what area are you going to trust God to help you this week? How can the rest of us pray for you?

12   Who in your life right now might you encourage with the hopeful message you're taking away from this session? If God gives you an opportunity, what do you want to tell them?

FREEDOM FROM WORRY
Overcoming Anxiety with God's Love, Purpose, and Power

Close the session in prayer. Pray for others in the group. Use the following prayer as you end this session:

Heavenly Father, my desire is to learn to trust You, to put my hope in You. Help me to lay down my fear and concern and to be more aware of Your presence. Thank You for caring for me. Thank You for accepting me, inconsistencies and all. Holy Spirit, guide my steps. May my heart be open to Your direction. In Jesus' name, amen.

Prayer Requests:

_____

_____

_____

_____

_____

_____

_____

_____

_____

_____

_____

_____

_____

_____

_____

_____

_____

_____

___

Going Deeper Bible Study
Personal Devotion & Reflection

You can explore the following Bible passages behind the teaching for this session as a group (if there is time) or on your own between sessions.

Read John 21:15-22. A couple of weeks after Jesus' death and resurrection, Peter was still struggling with the reality that he had denied knowing Christ. In His own time, Jesus pulled him aside after a shore breakfast in Galilee and gently reinstated him to service. John witnessed the conversation.

- How do you think the three rounds of "do you love me—feed My sheep" take Peter through a process of restoration that paralleled his three rounds of denial during Jesus' trial (see John 18:15-27)?

- When Jesus gave Peter a glimpse of how his life would end (John 21:18-19), Peter noticed John close by and asked, *Lord, what about him?* Note Jesus' answer again. Why is it more important to follow Christ than to know how your life or someone else's life is going to turn out?

FREEDOM FROM WORRY
Overcoming Anxiety with God's Love, Purpose, and Power

- Three years earlier, Jesus called Peter into discipleship. Read Mark 1:16-18 and compare Jesus' first command with His last command for Peter in John 21:22.

Read Psalm 19:1-14. One of the objectives of this session on *Freedom from Worry* was to learn to pray. David's psalm offers many sample prayers and lessons in prayer. This psalm ends with a strong series of prayers regarding self-examination, which is part of the listening discipline of prayer.

- Note that there is a change of audience in this psalm. Who's the audience in verses 1-10? Who's listening in verses 11-14? You can see this same pattern in Psalm 23. What is it about the subject of the psalm that causes David to make this shift?

- Verses 12-13 include three different kinds of sins. What are they, and how is each unique?

- How does David "cast each care" about sin in his life onto the Lord? How often would you say your worries flow out of fears about failure, mistakes, and sin? What help does this psalm offer you?

Daily Reflections

These are daily reviews of the key Bible verses and related Scriptures that will help you think about and apply the insights from this session.

Day 1 – 1 Timothy 6:6-8
The Pursuit of Contentment

But godliness with contentment is great gain. For we brought nothing into the world, and we can take nothing out of it. But if we have food and clothing, we will be content with that.

Reflection Question: How would you explain to someone the difference between contentment and complacency?

Day 2 – Matthew 6:24
One Master

"No one can serve two masters. Either he will hate the one and love the other, or he will be devoted to the one and despise the other. You cannot serve both God and Money."

Reflection Question: How do you know who or what you are actually serving in life?

Day 3 – Philippians 4:12
Contentment Learned

I know what it is to be in need, and I know what it is to have plenty. I have learned the secret of being content in any and every situation, whether well fed or hungry, whether living in plenty or in want.

Reflection Question: What specific situations in your life are potential training grounds for contentment?

Jesus answered, "If I want him to remain alive until I return, what is that to you? You must follow me."
Reflection Question: What did I do today that was an expression of following Jesus?

Day 5 – Hebrews 4:15-16
God Knows

For we do not have a high priest who is unable to sympathize with our weaknesses, but we have one who has been tempted in every way, just as we are—yet was without sin. Let us then approach the throne of grace with confidence, so that we may receive mercy and find grace to help us in our time of need.
Reflection Question: How does Jesus' understanding by experience encourage you to pray more openly?

Weekly Memory Verse:
Let us then approach the throne of grace with confidence, so that we may receive mercy and find grace to help us in our time of need.
(Hebrews 4:16)

Session 5

Our Reality

In this next-to-last session we begin to take the long look ahead. We don't get over dealing with issues that can cause worry. Every day is a fresh set of lessons, not so much in avoiding worry, but in trusting God. As Colossians 2:6-7 puts it, "So then, just as you received Christ Jesus as Lord, continue to live in him, rooted and built up in him, strengthened in the faith as you were taught, and overflowing with thankfulness."

Story

Kathy Nobles & Rachel Bunn

Rachel Bunn, first diagnosed at birth with cystic fibrosis and a two-year life expectancy, has lived more than thirty years in a daily struggle with the disease. Her favorite thought when it comes to the reality of her relationship with God is, "God has given me everything I need for today." She echoes the spirit of Jesus' words on how to overcome worry. We can't be anxious about what will happen next; we must focus on what God is doing, and can do, now.

Rachel and her mother, Kathy, have shared this rocky road and do not hesitate to admit the way has been hard. But they are quick to add that God has also been faithful. They understand and eloquently speak about the challenges of seeing God's presence in the moment, but they know from well-worn experience that tomorrow will allow them the opportunity to look back and see God's faithfulness in the midst of everything. They know what doesn't make sense today will make perfect sense tomorrow—or whenever God chooses to make it clear.

The nature of Rachel's and her brother's disease makes each day somewhat uncertain. Regular hospital visits mean other aspects of life are a little hard to plan, but somehow they have seen God make a way. They have experienced the powerful, intimate, day-by-day empowering of the Holy Spirit as God's personal involvement in their lives.

Kathy has thrived despite the continual challenge of having two children with medical needs. She has endured them being misunderstood and mistreated because they were different. At the same time, she has succeeded in maintaining a prosperous business while watching her children reach adulthood—an amazing miracle in itself, due to their medical condition.

But, as we will see, and must learn in our own lives, God's timing isn't ours. He rarely works instantly, but always perfectly. All things work together for good to those who love Him, and God has given us everything we need for today.

Getting Started

We will begin each session with a question or brief activity designed to "put us on the same page." Continue to make sure everyone knows each other's names.

1. Men and women often have very different interests and hobbies, but almost everything we do involves tools specific to that activity. What would be an example or two of unusual tools you have acquired for a specialized purpose?

2. When it comes to our spiritual lives, what tools would you say every Christian ought to have "in their box" for regular use?

FREEDOM FROM WORRY
Overcoming Anxiety with God's Love, Purpose, and Power

DVD Session #5

Throughout the sessions in *Freedom from Worry* we're hearing some pointed teaching from Pastor Allen Jackson as well as some personal stories from people like Kathy Nobles and Rachel Bunn, who are making strides on the worry-free journey. No matter where we are in the challenge to unload worry and not accumulate any more of it, we can definitely make progress with God's help and the encouragement of others. With that possibility in mind, let's begin our teaching for this session.

I. Our Reality

Romans 12:21
²¹ Do not be overcome by evil, but overcome evil with good.

1 Kings 19:14-18
¹⁴ He replied, "I have been very zealous for the LORD God Almighty. The Israelites have rejected your covenant, torn down your altars, and put your prophets to death with the sword. I am the only one left, and now they are trying to kill me too."

¹⁵ The LORD said to him, "Go back the way you came, and go to the Desert of Damascus. When you get there, anoint Hazael king over Aram.

¹⁶"Also, anoint Jehu son of Nimshi king over Israel, and anoint Elisha son of Shaphat from Abel Meholah to succeed you as prophet.

¹⁷"Jehu will put to death any who escape the sword of Hazael, and Elisha will put to death any who escape the sword of Jehu.

¹⁸"Yet I reserve seven thousand in Israel—all whose knees have not bowed down to Baal and whose mouths have not kissed him."

    A. Life is _____

B. You can be _____

C. Shrinking _____
is a state of mind that does not include
the majesty, power, and love of God the
Father. *This kind of mentality is a malady that
overtakes us in small steps.* We concede one
point after another, day after day, until finally
all hope is lost that life could be any different
than our immediate circumstances. (The frog
in the kettle!). The end result is despondency,
hopelessness, and self-absorption.

II. Endurance

A. Warnings

Hebrews 12:2-3
*² Let us fix our eyes on Jesus, the author and
perfecter of our faith, who for the joy set before
him endured the cross, scorning its shame, and
sat down at the right hand of the throne of
God.*

*³ Consider him who endured such opposition
from sinful men, so that you will not grow
weary and lose heart.*

Galatians 6:9
*⁹ Let us not become weary in doing good, for at
the proper time we will reap a harvest if we do
not give up.*

B. Hopelessness is a _____ problem.

Acts 27:20
*⁹ When neither sun nor stars appeared for many days and the storm
continued raging, we finally gave up all hope of being saved.*

Discussion

Using the questions that follow, we will review and expand on the teaching we just experienced. If time is limited, discuss bold questions first.

3 **What example(s) from your life would you use to illustrate the reality of worry-producing events, big or small, similar to Pastor Allen's story about the church building project?**

4 We reviewed the story of Elijah in the aftermath of the great showdown with the prophets of Baal in 1 Kings 19. How would you explain the odd change in Elijah, from a prophet who could call down God's fire from heaven to a cowering refugee feeling sorry for himself in the wilderness? How do you relate to that kind of shift?

5 **The first observation is that life is difficult. Even when yielded to the Lord, difficulties come. Jesus brings hope to our difficulties. Share an experience or two.**

6 What tools do Christians have when facing the challenges life brings?

7 We visited Hebrews 12:2-3 back in the first session and talked about Jesus as an example: *Let us fix our eyes on Jesus, the author and perfecter of our faith, who for the joy set before him endured the cross, scorning its shame, and sat down at the right hand of the throne of God. Consider him who endured such opposition from sinful men, so that you will not grow weary and lose heart.* What examples of endurance do you see in these verses?

8 Hopelessness settles upon us bit by bit until it becomes unbearable. The apostle Paul found himself in the midst of a group of people who were hopeless. How did a God-perspective give Paul a different outlook?

Application

Now it's time to make some personal applications of all we've been thinking about in the last few minutes.

9 **Pastor Allen said that problems and pressures tend to reduce space in our lives because we become so focused on our own immediate pain and discomfort. How have you found this true in your life?**

10 **How have Kathy and Rachel learned to enlarge the space in their lives even when it was under pressure to shrink back because of the disease? In what area of your life do you know you need to apply the same truth?**

FREEDOM FROM WORRY

Overcoming Anxiety with God's Love, Purpose, and Power

11 What are the steps we can take to make sure we don't miss the promise of Galatians 6:9 because we have given up?

12 How have you found studying *Freedom from Worry* with others a better way than alone to approach a significant issue in life?

13 Describe one relationship in your circle that has changed significantly as you have gained new freedoms from worry.

Close the session in prayer. Pray for others in the group. Use the following prayer as you end this session:

Heavenly Father, I rejoice today because You are my provider. I am Your child, and You are aware of all my needs. I thank You that You are Lord over my circumstances; Your grace and power are sufficient to meet all my concerns. Today I give You all my anxiety and frustration. I choose Your peace. Holy Spirit, help me to be content, to trust and to yield to Almighty God. I choose to turn my thoughts toward the majestic Kingdom of my Lord and rest in His provision. In Jesus' name, amen.

Prayer Requests:

_____

_____

_____

_____

_____

_____

_____

_____

_____

_____

Going Deeper Bible Study
Personal Devotion & Reflection

You can explore the following Bible passages behind the teaching for this session as a group (if there is time) or on your own between sessions.

Read Acts 27:1-26. The use of "we" and "us" in this passage reminds us that Doctor Luke was with Paul during much of his journey that began in Acts 20 in Ephesus, when Paul was told that suffering waited for him in Jerusalem and beyond. But Luke's eyewitness account is obvious in Acts 27:1. What Paul experienced on this leg of the journey was shared by Luke.

- From the time of Paul's "protective custody" arrest in Jerusalem (Acts 22) to his departure from Caesarea, over two years had passed. Paul went through three trials (Felix in Acts 24, Festus in Acts 25, and Agrippa in Acts 25-26). How do you relate to the connection between delay and the temptation to worry?

- As you scan this passage in Acts 27, what were the main events that encroached on the confidence of the crew and passengers on Paul's ship?

- Read verse 20 again. How does a progressive and relentless series of negative events affect you? Given your own experiences, do you think God is more interested in changing our circumstances for the better or in changing us so we can endure what we encounter in life? Why?

FREEDOM FROM WORRY
Overcoming Anxiety with God's Love, Purpose, and Power

- What role did Paul's words in verses 21-26 play, and what message would you draw from them that would apply to any "hopeless" situation?

Read 1 Kings 18:16 -19:18. If you haven't studied or read the showdown between Elijah and the prophets of Baal in a while, the details of the story are fascinating. We won't appreciate the kind of personal vulnerability we've mentioned in the last couple of sessions unless we can see how it plays out in the life of someone like Elijah. Elijah alone was in big trouble; Elijah and God were triumphant.

- Looking at the whole story, what was the turning point between Elijah, God's man on the spot, and Elijah, man on the run? What factors can you see that might have made Elijah vulnerable to fear and worry, despite his recent victory?

- How would you illustrate "shrinking thinking" from Elijah's experience on the run?

- Skim the story again and note the sequence from the beginning of everything God did for Elijah as the events unfolded. What personal hope would you take from the way God handled Elijah?

Daily Reflections

These are daily reviews of the key Bible verses and related Scriptures that will help you think about and apply the insights from this session.

Day 1 – Romans 12:21
Enduring for Good
Do not be overcome by evil, but overcome evil with good.
Reflection Question: How prepared are you to do good today?

Day 2 – Galatians 6:9
Look for a Harvest
Let us not become weary in doing good, for at the proper time we will reap a harvest if we do not give up.
Reflection Question: How do you combat weariness?

Day 3 – Revelation 12:11
Ultimate Endurance
They overcame him by the blood of the Lamb and by the word of their testimony; they did not love their lives so much as to shrink from death.
Reflection Question: How do you keep from thinking you have to endure/overcome in your own strength?

Day 4 – Acts 27:20

Standing in the Storm

When neither sun nor stars appeared for many days and the storm continued raging, we finally gave up all hope of being saved.

Reflection Question: How do you plan to handle a long storm in life?

Day 5 – James 1:2-4

Growing Endurance

Consider it pure joy, my brothers, whenever you face trials of many kinds, because you know that the testing of your faith develops perseverance. Perseverance must finish its work so that you may be mature and complete, not lacking anything.

Reflection Question: How is your faith being tested this week in order to grow your endurance?

Weekly Memory Verse:

Let us not become weary in doing good, for at the proper time we will reap a harvest if we do not give up.

Galatians 6:9

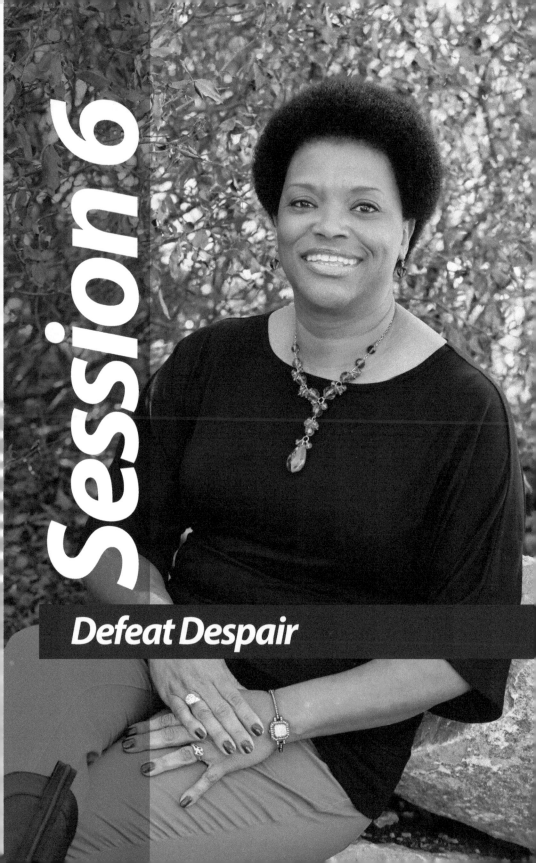

Session 6

Defeat Despair

In this final session Pastor Allen continues to define some lifelong tools that can be used repeatedly to take action against the tide of hopelessness and despair that will rise against us from time to time. The challenges and difficulties in life are seldom avoidable. A tempting detour is usually just the way into different difficulties. But there are certain multipurpose spiritual tools that will carry us a long way in defeating despair.

Story

Robin Young

When we stand as young people at our wedding altar and say to each other, among other things, "'til death do us part," it's actually hard to imagine what that means. We are probably healthy and assume we have a long life ahead of us. We don't really want, in that moment, to think about the deep truth that life on this side of eternity will have a stopping point. In all likelihood, one of us at the wedding altar will lay the other in the grave.

Robin Young knows how much that hurts. She knows the delight of a childhood love, which led to an adult relationship that lasted almost three decades until a nightmarish diagnosis and a long final struggle to death from cancer. She knows how God walked her through that dark valley for His purposes in her life. As she puts it, she had to learn to shift all of her dependence on her husband, Michael, over to God.

For her, dealing with worry is a daily decision to trust God despite whatever she's facing. She clearly remembers a childhood filled with watching a mother who worried way too much and died way too young. She determined that the way to avoid that path was to trust God, even when it was hard—especially when it was hard.

Two surprises have delighted Robin in the years since Michael's death: the way God has met her needs, and the way she has learned to love people. In fact, she says the first thing she wants to tell Michael when they meet in Heaven is, "When you left, I got your passion for others. Thanks for teaching me how to love people!"

Great tragedies and disappointments in life certainly can cause us to be very angry at God. Robin smiles and says, "I understand, because I've been there. But I don't stay there long." God accepts anger as an initial reaction, but it's not a helpful long-term response. Lean into the Body of Christ, and discover that good things can come out of the worst times in life.

Getting Started

We've said more than once during these sessions that all the wisdom about worry and all the tools for handling anxiety aren't worth much if we don't use them.

1. What have you discovered during these sessions of *Freedom from Worry* that you believe will make a difference in your life going forward?

2. Given the experience we've had in these sessions, what are some other topics or questions you would like to see our small group address at some point in the future?

3. Review your Small Group Agreement on page 86 and evaluate how well you met your goals.

DVD Session #6

Throughout the sessions in *Freedom from Worry* we're hearing some pointed teaching from Pastor Allen Jackson as well as some personal stories from people like Robin Young, whose life can teach us about *Freedom from Worry*. Their stories are for our encouragement. Let's begin our teaching for this session.

I. Defeat Despair

A. Consider the _____

Romans 8:31-32
31 What, then, shall we say in response to this? If God is for us, who can be against us?

32 He who did not spare his own Son, but gave him up for us all—how will he not also, along with him, graciously give us all things?

1. Admission of _____

2. Demonstration of God's _____

B. In the presence of _____

Isaiah 41:10-13
10"So do not fear, for I am with you; do not be dismayed, for I am your God. I will strengthen you and help you; I will uphold you with my righteous right hand.

11"All who rage against you will surely be ashamed and disgraced; those who oppose you will be as nothing and perish.

¹²*"Though you search for your enemies, you will not find them. Those who wage war against you will be as nothing at all.*

¹³*"For I am the LORD, your God, who takes hold of your right hand and says to you, Do not fear; I will help you."*

1. Tell God exactly how you _____

2. Acknowledge a willingness to _____

3. _____ for who He is and for what He has done.

4. Ask Him to _____ my life

C. Daily feed the _____ of hope

Proverbs 3:25-26
²⁵ *Have no fear of sudden disaster or of the ruin that overtakes the wicked,*

²⁶ *for the LORD will be your confidence and will keep your foot from being snared.*

D. Take time to _____

Psalm 37:4
⁴ *Delight yourself in the LORD and he will give you the desires of your heart.*

E. Forget our _____ and
_____ others

FREEDOM FROM WORRY
Overcoming Anxiety with God's Love, Purpose, and Power

1 Samuel 8:6-7
⁶ But when they said, "Give us a king to lead us," this displeased Samuel; so he prayed to the LORD.

⁷ And the LORD told him: "Listen to all that the people are saying to you; it is not you they have rejected, but they have rejected me as their king."

F. Remember the _____

Hebrews 11:5
⁵ By faith Enoch was . . . commended as one who pleased God.

Discussion

Using the questions that follow, we will review and expand on the teaching we just experienced. If time is limited, discuss bold questions first.

4 **On the cross, Jesus exhausted the curse of sin and made available the blessing of His righteousness. How does it make you feel to know you don't have to earn God's blessings?**

5 Pastor Allen suggested that we can defeat despair by letting a single passage of Scripture wash over us repeatedly. How do you use the Bible to spend time in God's presence?

6 The phrase "live the truth you know" reminds us not to get sidetracked on matters of curiosity rather than trusting God with the matters of life. What is one truth you live with almost every day?

7 What are some of the ways you know you can daily feed the sparks of hope? These may not necessarily be obvious or traditional devotional practices, but what fuels hope for you?

8 **Taking time to dream may sound a little odd, but Psalm 37:4 offers some context: Delight yourself in the Lord, and he will give you the desires of your heart. How do you fill your mind with thoughts about God?**

FREEDOM FROM WORRY

Overcoming Anxiety with God's Love, Purpose, and Power

9 Forgetting failures and forgiving others may feel like a tandem of impossibilities, but every time we pray the Lord's Prayer we invite God to treat us as we treat others. Which of those two tools do you most need to learn to use better?

10 Pastor Allen used Hebrews 11:5 to remind us that our ultimate goal is to please God. What do you intentionally do regularly that you know pleases your Heavenly Father?

Application

At this point we move in our discussion from talking about implications of the teaching to application of the teaching. If we grasp what the idea means we can talk about what it means in our lives.

11 How would you say your personal understanding and commitment to living a worry-free life has been affected by this study?

12 Before we complete our study, let's take a minute and practice forgiveness. Identify a disappointment or painful season in your life. Identify the people or organizations involved with the hurt. Take a courageous step and say this simple prayer:

Heavenly Father, I forgive _____.
I set them free today from any obligation, from any need of apology or restitution. I thank you that you forgive me. In Jesus' name, amen.

13 Take a few minutes to jot down three specific action steps that would move you further on the journey toward a worry-free life. You may want to look back over the earlier lesson outlines.

a. _____

b. _____

c. _____

14 Now share at least one of these, if not all three, with the rest of the group to create a point of accountability. Give the group permission to ask you about your progress in this or these steps.

Close the session in prayer. Pray for others in the group. Use the following prayer as you end this session:

Heavenly Father, today I choose a new beginning. Forgive me for refusing Your comfort and authority. I choose to yield to Your best. I trust You to lead me through each challenge. I will rejoice in Your faithfulness. Holy Spirit, help me to receive all that God intends. In Jesus' name, amen.

Prayer Requests:

_____
_____
_____
_____
_____
_____
_____
_____
_____
_____

FREEDOM FROM WORRY

Overcoming Anxiety with God's Love, Purpose, and Power

Going Deeper Bible Study
Personal Devotion & Reflection

You can explore the following Bible passages behind the teaching for this session as a group (if there is time) or on your own between sessions.

Read Psalm 1:1-6. The first psalm gives us an overview of the two kinds of lives people live. One is healthy and tree-like, producing fruit in season. The other is chaff-like and blown away by the lightest wind. Do we know how to pursue the life we want?

- What are the three sources of input that someone should avoid when developing a blessed life? How do they differ from each other?

- What does it mean to you to delight in God's Word? And how does delighting lead to meditating on Scripture?

- What does this phrase from verse 6 mean to you: "For the LORD watches over the way of the righteous"?

Read Psalm 40:1-5. In this passage, the psalmist is meditating on his relationship with God leading to a direct statement to God. This sense of God hovering and attentive in our lives is a big part of what it means to practice His presence.

- In what ways do the first three verses express a profound testimony by someone who recognizes God's work in their life?

- How does verse 4 contrast the source of blessing in our lives with the source of hopelessness?

- Take a few minutes and brainstorm together some of what the psalmist might have had in mind by the phrases, "wonders you have done" and "things you planned for us" as ways of acknowledging God's presence?

Daily Reflections

These are daily reviews of the key Bible verses and related Scriptures that will help you think about and apply the insights from this session.

Day 1 – Psalm 1:2

Practicing the Presence of God

But his delight is in the law of the LORD, and on his law he meditates day and night.

Reflection Question: What part of God's Word gives you most delight these days?

Day 2 – Romans 8:31-32

An Admirable Gift

What, then, shall we say in response to this? If God is for us, who can be against us? He who did not spare his own Son, but gave him up for us all— how will he not also, along with him, graciously give us all things?

Reflection Question: As you consider the cross, how does the truth that God is for you change your outlook on worrisome things?

Day 3 – Proverbs 3:25-26

God in Place of Worry

Have no fear of sudden disaster or of the ruin that overtakes the wicked, for the LORD will be your confidence and will keep your foot from being snared.

Reflection Question: How do you think your life would be different if the Lord really was your confidence?

"For I am the LORD, your God, who takes hold of your right hand and says to you, Do not fear; I will help you."
Reflection Question: How does the promise of God's help confront your fears?

Day 5 – Psalm 37:4
Delight before Desires
Delight yourself in the LORD and he will give you the desires of your heart.
Reflection Question: Are you willing to learn to delight yourself in the Lord and see Him give you the desires of your heart? What keeps you from worry-free living?

Weekly Memory Verse:
What, then, shall we say in response to this? If God is for us, who can be against us? He who did not spare his own Son, but gave him up for us all—how will he not also, along with him, graciously give us all things?

Romans 8:31-32

Appendix

Great resources to help make your small group experience even better!

Frequently Asked Questions

What do we do on the first night of our group?

Like all fun things in life–have a party! A "get to know you" coffee, dinner, or dessert is a great way to launch a new study. You may

want to review the Small Group Agreement (page 86) and share the names of a few friends you can invite to join you. But most importantly, have fun before your study time begins.

Where do we find new members for our group?

We encourage you to pray with your group and then brainstorm a list of people from work, church, your neighborhood, your children's school, family, the gym, and so forth. Then have each group member invite several of the people on his or her list.

No matter how you find participants, it's vital that you stay on the lookout for new people to join your group. All groups tend to go through healthy attrition–the result of moves, releasing new leaders, ministry opportunities, and so forth–and if the group gets too small, it could be at risk of shutting down. If you and your group stay open, you'll be amazed at the people God sends your way. The next person just might become a friend for life. You never know!

How long will this group meet?

It's totally up to the group–once you come to the end of this six-week study. Most groups meet weekly for at least their first six weeks, but every other week can work as well.

FREEDOM FROM WORRY
Overcoming Anxiety with God's Love, Purpose, and Power

At the end of this study, each group member may decide if he or she wants to continue on for another six-week study. Some groups launch relationships for years to come, and others are stepping-stones into another group experience. Either way, enjoy the journey.

What if this group is not working for us?

You're not alone! This could be the result of a personality conflict, life stage difference, geographical distance, level of spiritual maturity, or any number of things. Relax. Pray for God's direction, and at the end of this six-week study, decide whether to continue with this group or find another. You don't buy the first car you look at or marry the first person you date, and the same goes with a group. Don't bail out before the six weeks are up– God might have something to teach you. Also, don't run from conflict or prejudge people before you have given them a chance. God is still working in you too!

How do we handle the childcare needs in our group?

We suggest that you empower the group to openly brainstorm solutions. You may try one option that works for a while and then adjust over time. Our favorite approach is for adults to meet in the living room or dining room, and to share the cost of a babysitter (or two) who can be with the kids in a different part of the house. In this way, parents don't have to be away from their children all evening when their children are too young to be left at home. A second option is to use one home for the kids and a second home (close by or a phone call away) for the adults. A third idea is to rotate the responsibility of providing a lesson or care for the children either in the same home or in another home nearby. This can be an incredible blessing for kids. Finally, the most common idea is to decide that you need to have a night to invest in your spiritual lives individually or as a couple, and to make your own arrangements for child care. No matter what decision the group makes, the best approach is to dialogue openly about both the problem and the solution.

Small Group Agreement

Our Expectations:

To provide a predictable environment where participants experience authentic community and spiritual growth.

Group Attendance	To give priority to the group meeting. We will call or email if we will be late or absent. (Completing the Group Calendar will minimize this issue.)
Safe Environment	To help create a safe place where people can be heard and feel loved. (Please, no quick answers, snap judgments, or simple fixes.)
Respect Differences	To be gentle and gracious to people with different spiritual maturity, personal opinions, temperaments, or "imperfections" in fellow group members. We are all works in progress.
Confidentiality	To keep anything that is shared strictly confidential and within the group, and to avoid sharing improper information about those outside the group.
Encouragement for Growth	To be not just takers but givers of life. We want to spiritually multiply our life by serving others with our God-given gifts.
Shared Ownership	To remember that every member is a minister and to ensure that each attender will share a small team role or responsibility over time.

Our Times Together:

• Refreshments _____

• Childcare _____

• When we will meet (day of week) _____

• Where we will meet (place) _____

• We will begin at (time) _____ and end at _____

• We will do our best to have some or all of us attend a worship service together.

   Our primary worship service time will be _____

• Date of this agreement _____

• Date we will review this agreement again _____

• Who (other than the leader) will review this agreement at the end of this

   study _____

Small Group Calendar

Date	Lesson	Host Home	Refreshments	Leader
11/16	1	Steve and Laura's	Joe	Bill

FREEDOM FROM WORRY
Overcoming Anxiety with God's Love, Purpose, and Power

Memory Verses

Session 1

Do not be anxious about anything, but in everything, by prayer and petition, with thanksgiving, present your requests to God.
Philippians 4:6

Session 2

But seek first his kingdom and his righteousness, and all these things will be given to you as well. Therefore do not worry about tomorrow, for tomorrow will worry about itself. Each day has enough trouble of its own.
Matthew 6:33-34

Session 3

Above all else, guard your heart, for it is the wellspring of life.
Proverbs 4:23

Session 4

Let us then approach the throne of grace with confidence, so that we may receive mercy and find grace to help us in our time of need.
Hebrews 4:16

Session 5

Let us not become weary in doing good, for at the proper time we will reap a harvest if we do not give up.
Galatians 6:9

Session 6

What, then, shall we say in response to this? If God is for us, who can be against us? He who did not spare his own Son, but gave him up for us all--how will he not also, along with him, graciously give us all things?
Romans 8:31-32

Prayer and Praise Report

	Prayer Requests	Praise Reports
Session 1		
Session 2		
Session 3		
Session 4		
Session 5		
Session 6		

FREEDOM FROM WORRY

Overcoming Anxiety with God's Love, Purpose, and Power

Small Group Roster

NAME	PHONE	EMAIL

Small Group Leaders

Key resources to help your leadership
experience be the best it can be

Hosting an Open House

If you're starting a new group, try planning an "open house" before your first formal group meeting. Even if you only have two to four core

members, it's a great way to break the ice and to consider prayerfully who else might be open to joining you over the next few weeks. You can also use this kick-off meeting to hand out study guides, spend some time getting to know each other, discuss each person's expectations for the group, and briefly pray for each other.

A simple meal or good desserts always make a kick-off meeting more fun. After people introduce themselves and share how they ended up being at the meeting (you can play a game to see who has the wildest story!), have everyone respond to a few icebreaker questions: "What is your favorite family vacation?" or "What is one thing you love about your church/our community?" or "What are three things about your life growing up that most people here don't know?" Next, ask everyone to tell what they hope to get out of the study. You might want to review the Small Group Agreement and talk about each person's expectations and priorities.

Finally, set an empty chair (maybe two) in the center of your group and explain that it represents someone who would enjoy or benefit from this group but who isn't here yet. Ask people to pray about whom they could invite to join the group over the next few weeks. Hand out post-cards and have everyone write an invitation or two. Don't worry about ending up with too many people; you can always have one discussion circle in the living room and another in the dining room after you watch the lesson. Each group could then report prayer requests and progress at the end of the session.

You can skip this kick-off meeting if your time is limited, but you'll experience a huge benefit if you take the time to connect with each other in this way.

Leading for the First Time

- Sweaty palms are a healthy sign. The Bible says God is gracious to the humble. Remember who is in control; if you feel inadequate, that is probably a good sign. Those who are soft in heart (and sweaty palmed) are those whom God is sure to speak through.

- Seek support. Ask your leader, coleader, or close friend to pray for you and prepare with you before the session. Walking through the study will help you anticipate potentially difficult questions and discussion topics.

- Bring your uniqueness to the study. Lean into who you are and how God wants you to uniquely lead the study.

- Prepare. Prepare. Prepare. Go through the session several times. If you are using the DVD, listen to the teaching segment and Leadership Lifter. Consider writing in a journal or fasting for a day to prepare yourself for what God wants to do.

- Ask for feedback so you can grow. Perhaps in an email or on cards handed out at the study, have everyone write down three things you did well and one thing you could improve on. Don't get defensive, but show an openness to learn and grow.

- Use online resources. Go to allenjackson.com to order additional study guides and other materials.

- Prayerfully consider launching a new group. This doesn't need to happen overnight, but God's heart is for this to happen over time. Not all Christians are called to be leaders or teachers, but we are all called to be "shepherds" of a few someday.

- Share with your group what God is doing in your heart. God is searching for those whose hearts are fully His. Share your trials and victories. We promise that people will relate.

FREEDOM FROM WORRY

Overcoming Anxiety with God's Love, Purpose, and Power

Leadership Training 101

Congratulations! You have responded to the call to help shepherd Jesus' flock. There are few other tasks in the family of God that surpass the contribution you will be making. As you prepare to lead, whether it is one session or the entire series, here are a few thoughts to keep in mind. We encourage you to read these and review them with each new discussion leader before he or she leads.

1 **Remember that you are not alone.** God knows everything about you, and He knew that you would be asked to lead your group. Remember that it is common for all good leaders to feel that they are not ready to lead. Moses, Solomon, Jeremiah, and Timothy – they all were reluctant to lead. God promises, "Never will I leave you; never will I forsake you." (Hebrews 13:5) Whether you are leading for one evening, for several weeks, or for a lifetime, you will be blessed as you serve.

2 **Don't try to do it alone.** Pray right now for God to help you build a healthy leadership team. If you can enlist a coleader to help you lead the group, you will find your experience to be much richer. This is your chance to involve as many people as you can in building a healthy group. All you have to do is call and ask people to help. You'll be surprised at the response.

3 **Just be yourself.** If you won't be you, who will? God wants you to use your unique gifts and temperament. Don't try to do things exactly like another leader; do them in a way that fits you! Just admit it when you don't have an answer, and apologize when you make a mistake. Your group will love you for it, and you'll sleep better at night!

Prepare for your meeting ahead of time. Review the session and the leader's notes, and write down your responses to each question. Pay special attention to exercises that ask group members to do something other than engage in discussion.

These exercises will help your group live what the Bible teaches, not just talk about it. Be sure you understand how an exercise works, and bring any necessary supplies (such as paper and pens) to your meeting. If the exercise employs one of the items in the appendix, be sure to look over that item so you'll know how it works. Finally, review "Outline for Each Session" so you'll remember the purpose of each section in the study.

Pray for your group members by name. Before you begin your session, go around the room in your mind and pray for each member by name. You may want to review the prayer list at least once a week. Ask God to use your time together to touch the heart of every person uniquely. Expect God to lead you to whomever He wants you to encourage or challenge in a special way. If you listen, God will surely lead!

When you ask a question, be patient. Someone will eventually respond. Sometimes people need a moment or two of silence to think about the question, and if silence doesn't bother you, it won't bother anyone else. After someone responds, affirm the response with a simple "thanks" or "good job." Then ask, "How about somebody else?" or "Would someone who hasn't shared like to add anything?" Be sensitive to new people or reluctant members who aren't ready to say, pray, or do anything. If you give them a safe setting, they will blossom over time.

Provide transitions between questions. When guiding the discussion, always read aloud the transitional paragraphs and the questions. Ask the group if anyone would like to read the paragraph or Bible passage. Don't call on anyone, but ask for a volunteer, and then be patient until someone begins. Be sure to thank the person who reads aloud.

FREEDOM FROM WORRY
Overcoming Anxiety with God's Love, Purpose, and Power

Break up into small groups each week, or they won't stay. If your group has more than seven people, we strongly encourage you to have the group gather sometimes in discussion circles of three or four people during the Discussion section of the study. With a greater opportunity to talk in a small circle, people will connect more with the study, apply more quickly what they're learning, and ultimately get more out of it. A small circle also encourages a quiet person to participate and tends to minimize the effects of a more vocal or dominant member. It can also help people feel more loved in your group. When you gather again at the end of the section, you can have one person summarize the highlights from each circle. Small circles are also helpful during prayer time. People who are unaccustomed to praying aloud will feel more comfortable trying it with just two or three others. Also, prayer requests won't take as much time, so circles will have more time to actually pray. When you gather back with the whole group, you can have one person from each circle briefly update everyone on the prayer requests. People are more willing to pray in small circles if they know that the whole group will hear all the prayer requests.

Final challenge: Before your first opportunity to lead, look up each of the five passages listed below. Read each one as a devotional exercise to help equip yourself with a shepherd's heart. Trust us on this one. If you do this, you will be more than ready for your first meeting.

Matthew 9:36
1 Peter 5:2-4
Psalm 23
Ezekiel 34:11-16
1 Thessalonians 2:7-8, 11-12

About the Author

Allen Jackson is passionate about helping people become Christ-followers who respond to God's invitations for their life. He has served World Outreach Church, which started as a home Bible study in his parents' home, since 1981. In 1989 he became senior pastor, and under his leadership, the church has grown to a congregation of over 15,000 through prayer, outreach activities, community events, and worship services designed to share the Gospel.

Allen Jackson Ministries broadcasts his timely biblical messages over television, radio, and the internet. They also publish his teachings as books, Bible studies, and other resources that are used across the United States and internationally.

Jackson has spoken at pastors' conferences in the United States and abroad. He has also been a featured speaker during Jerusalem's Feast of Tabernacles celebration for the Vision for Israel organization, and the International Christian Embassy Jerusalem.

With degrees from Oral Roberts University and Vanderbilt University, and additional studies at Gordon-Conwell Theological Seminary and Hebrew University of Jerusalem, Jackson is uniquely equipped to help people develop a love and understanding of God's Word.

Pastor Jackson's wife, Kathy, is an active participant in ministry at World Outreach Church.

FREEDOM FROM WORRY

OVERCOMING ANXIETY

WITH GOD'S LOVE PURPOSE & POWER

WRITTEN BY
G. ALLEN JACKSON

Do not be anxious about anything, but in everything, by prayer and petition, with thanksgiving, present your requests to God. And the peace of God, which transcends all understanding, will guard your hearts and your minds in Christ Jesus.

Philippians 4:6-7

Worry contends with every one of us. To move beyond it is to press into life with a renewed vision of who God is, and with a recognition of His strength and provision in our lives. We need to know what God says about us, and we need to believe it.

"Sometimes the worries and anxieties of life can become so overwhelming we fear our world could suddenly collapse around us at any moment. We tend to look so close at our problems before us that they seem more than we could possibly handle... taking a step back we can see that God is bigger than the mountain. We need to have a new God perspective. This book will guide you through the steps to overcome worry and learn to live free in Christ. Praise God!"

Jane Leuthmers

ALLEN JACKSON
MINISTRIES

P.O. BOX 331028 MURFREESBORO, TN 37133 • (844) 377-7057 • allenjackson.com

FREEDOM FROM WORRY

Overcoming Anxiety with God's Love, Purpose, and Power

FREEDOM FROM WORRY

Overcoming Anxiety with God's Love, Purpose, and Power